ARIANA GRANDE

ALPHABET

Words by Robin Feiner

Aa

A is for **A**rianators.
That's the special name Ariana gives her devoted fans — and yes, that means you! She loves you with all her heart.

13
THE MUSICAL

B is for Broadway.
At just 15, Ariana made her stage debut in 13: The Musical, playing a cheerleader named Charlotte. She sang, danced, and dazzled the audience as her wild journey began.

Cc

C is for Cat Valentine.
Cat was the sweet, silly girl Ariana played on Victorious and Sam & Cat. Who could resist her red hair, squeaky voice, and huge heart?

01
02
03
04
05
06
07
08
09
10
11
12
13
14
15
ARIANA GRANDE
DANGEROUS WOMAN

Dd

D is for Dangerous Woman. In 2016, Ariana dropped Dangerous Woman and proved just how powerful she could be. With bunny ears and big vocals, she made every song shine.

E

Ee

E is for Eternal Sunshine. Released in 2024, Eternal Sunshine is full of emotion, honesty, and dreamy melodies. It's totally unforgettable — just like Ari.

F

F is for Frankie.
Frankie Grande is Ariana's big brother and best friend since forever. They love to sing, dance, and light up the world together.

G is for Grammy.
Ariana won her very first Grammy in 2019 for her album Sweetener. Her speech was short and sweet — but her smile said it all.

H

Hh

H is for High Pony.
No one rocks a ponytail like Ariana — high, shiny, and fierce. It's not just a hairstyle, it's a whole attitude.

I is for Into You.
This song became a mega hit in 2016 with its sparkly beat and exciting energy. Fans couldn't stop dancing — or singing along.

J is for Just Like Magic. Ariana sings about thinking happy thoughts and making magic happen. It's a little song with a lot of sparkle — like casting your own spell.

K

K is for K Bye for Now.
In 2019, Ariana released this live album from her Sweetener World Tour. It's full of big moments and all the love from every show.

Ll

L is for Love Me Harder. This moody duet with The Weeknd came out in 2014 and became a huge hit. With every note, Ariana showed how beautiful her voice truly is.

M

Mm

M is for **M**akeup.
Ariana created her own beauty brand, r.e.m. beauty, in 2021. She wants fans to feel confident, creative, and totally themselves.

N

N is for **N**o Tears Left to Cry. After a tough time, Ariana returned in 2018 with this song of strength and hope. She reminds the world that even when you fall, you can rise — and sparkle again.

O is for One Last Time.
This heartfelt track became a favorite from her 2014 album My Everything. It's a song of love and remembrance that fans hold close.

P is for Positions.
In 2020, Ariana showed off her grown-up side with Positions. She sang about love, balance, and being the boss of her own world.

Q

Qq

Q is for Quit.
Ariana teamed up with Cashmere Cat in 2017 to create this dreamy, whisper-soft song. It's all about holding on with all you've got.

R

R is for Rain on Me.
Ariana and Lady Gaga joined forces in 2020 with this stormy, sparkly pop anthem. They danced through the rain and turned tears into power.

S

Ss

S is for Sweetener.
Released in 2018, Sweetener went straight to number one and won Ariana her first Grammy. It's full of soft sounds, big feelings, and songs that make you smile.

Tt

T is for Thank U, Next.
In 2018, Ariana sang about moving on with grace and loving what life teaches you. She turned her story into a song—and made it a movement.

U is for Stuck with U.
Ariana and Justin Bieber sang this sweet duet in 2020 during lockdown. It's all about love, patience, and being with someone who feels like home.

V is for Victorious.
Back in 2010, Ariana became a TV star as Cat Valentine on Victorious. She sang, she laughed, and fans instantly fell in love.

Ww

W is for Wicked.
Ariana's lifelong dream came true when she was cast as Glinda in the Wicked movies. She brings bubbles, sparkle, and a voice fit for Oz.

Xx

X is for X-mas.
Ariana's holiday songs like Santa Tell Me and Wit It This Christmas are full of cheer. They twinkle like lights and feel like fresh-baked cookies.

Y

Y is for Yours Truly.
This 2013 debut album introduced the world to Ariana's sweet voice and vintage R&B style. From the very first track, fans knew she was something special.

Z is for Zach Sang.
Ariana's favorite interviewer, Zach always brings out her real laugh and honest thoughts. Their chats are funny, friendly, and full of Arianator magic.

The ever-expanding legendary library

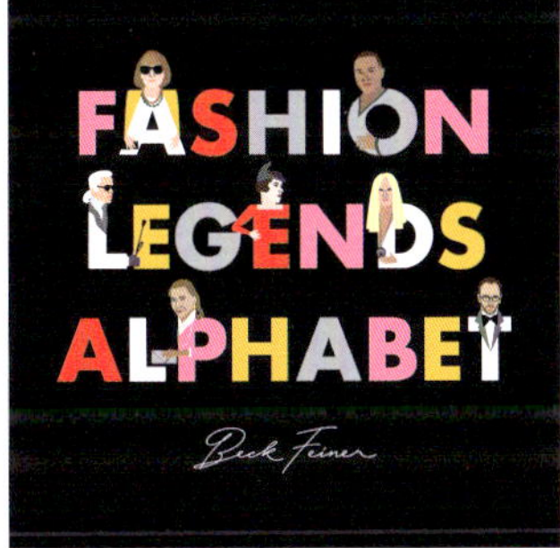

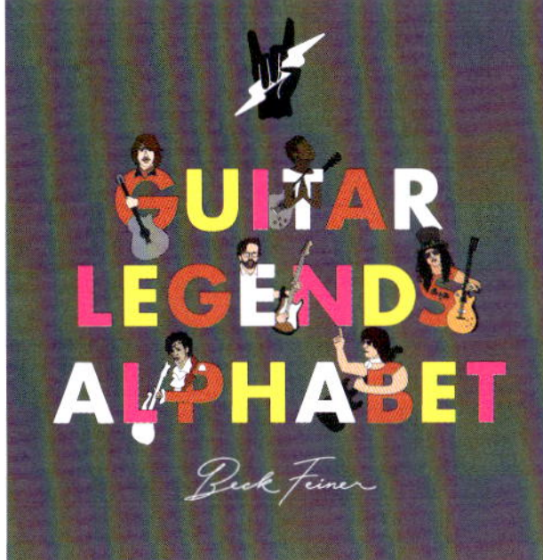

EXPLORE THESE LEGENDARY ALPHABETS & MORE AT WWW.ALPHABETLEGENDS.COM

ARIANA GRANDE ALPHABET
www.alphabetlegends.com

Published by Alphabet Legends Pty Ltd in 2025
Created by Beck Feiner

Printed and bound in China.

9781763865228